ODILON REDON

ODILON REDON

by JEAN SELZ

CROWN PUBLISHERS, INC. - NEW YORK

Translated from the French by:

EILEEN B. HENNESSY

LIBRARY OF CONGRESS CATALOG CARD NUMBER : 73-147349
PRINTED IN ITALY - © 1971 BY UFFICIPRESS, S.A. LUGANO
ALL RIGHTS IN THE U.S.A. ARE RESERVED BY CROWN PUBLISHERS INC., NEW YORK, N.Y.

BRETON PORT, 1879 or 1883   Oil, 8″ × 12½″   Arï Redon Collection, Paris

Of all the painters whose secrets are known to us, Odilon Redon was
the one who experienced the greatest difficulty – or used the greatest discretion
– in explaining his painting. However, he formulated a lucid definition of his art
by saying that it consisted of putting « the logic of the visible at the service of the
invisible. » His work does in fact occupy a place between sight and vision. Redon,
as much a narrator of the imagination as an observer of nature, shuttled from
one to the other with a steadfast desire to avoid breaking the bond that in his
eyes made them inseparable. But his activity was not always carried on exactly
in accordance with his definition: we could reverse the terms and say that he
also placed the resources of the invisible at the service of the visible. This dual
orientation of his mind, this movement back and forth over the same path

between the real and the unreal, explain that which constitutes at once the unity and the diversity of his output. After half a century, his work, which is sincere and exceptional – two words which cannot be dissociated in speaking of Redon – retains its power to rivet our gaze and arouse our curiosity.

A solitary apprenticeship

The road that led Redon to the threshold of what he himself modestly called « a small door opened onto the mystery » first crosses a half-savage landscape whose ancient trees, stones, and brambles, under the harsh sun or the abundant rains, were a source of unforgettable delights. This landscape surrounded the house at Peyrelebade, in the Médoc, where he spent his childhood, and which he very often mentioned in his writings with a fervor which never diminished. Its influence on the formation of his character and his mind was a continuation of the one later exerted on him by museums and books. For in the work of painters and poets he was first to seek the renewal of the emotions which a long intimacy with the scenes of nature, and the discovery of what nature contains in the way of the wondrous and the fantastic, had led him to experience. He was so fascinated by it that he was able to write in his *Notes* (published posthumously in a volume entitled *À Soi-même*): « My aptitude for contemplation made my search for a personal way of seeing things painful. »

Several factors in these years of Redon's youth – factors whose importance should be neither exaggerated nor belittled – are noteworthy. In particular, they seem like signs that help to make the progress of his destiny more intelligible to us.

For a child like Odilon Redon, timid, quiet, of almost morbid sensitivity, inclined to dreaminess and anxiety, the very attraction of that which was capable of disturbing him seems as it were a power of vertigo to which he surrendered with an anguished sensation of pleasure. «As a child I sought out the shadows,» he was later to write. « I remember taking a deep and unusual joy in hiding under the big curtains and in the dark corners of the house.» It was here in the old manor house at Peyrelebade that he was to produce all his *noirs*, his « black pictures, » as he called the more than five hundred charcoal drawings he left, and which constitute a major portion of his work.

For such a child, drawing was already a refuge in which his revulsion for all that was violent could be gratified. It was the act by which he took full possession of his solitude – the second act, after that of contemplation. It is not surprising that, in 1851, at the age of eleven, he received a prize for drawing. Four years earlier he had spent some time in Paris, and from this visit he retained the memory of his first visits to the museums. « An impression of the

Flight, around 1865   India-ink wash, 11¾″ × 18″
Kröller-Möller Rijksmuseum, Otterloo, The Netherlands

paintings of dramatic scenes has remained in my memory. My eyes are full of nothing but depictions of violent life, of an excess of life; that was the only thing which struck me. »

Around the age of fifteen he had a drawing teacher, a pupil of Isabey named Stanislas Gorin, whose studio, in the middle of a garden with an abundance of flowers, was located in a suburb of Bordeaux. In Redon's own words, he was a « distinguished painter of watercolors » but, he adds, « romantic and enthusiastic » as well, and he seems to have been an excellent teacher for Redon, being careful to develop his pupil's sensitivity of observation and to respect his personal inclinations. Young Redon was beginning to become interested in the Bordeaux Museum and in the major exhibitions being held at that time in the city. Among the painters who were to attract his attention to the greatest degree, three names appear to us to be particularly significant: those of Delacroix, Corot, and Gustave Moreau.

Redon made copies of Delacroix's works, and his admiration for that artist was to appear frequently in his writings and sometimes in his work. In 1878 he analyzed several canvases of the painter to whom, by his own admission, he owed his « first awakening » and the permanence of his «own flame.» His favorite was the *Chariot of Apollo,* a theme which he himself was to depict several times in a very personal manner after abandoning his *noirs* for color. What he says of Delacroix's composition could accurately be applied to his own: « It is the triumph of light over the shadows, the joy of broad daylight opposed to the sorrows of the night and the shadows. » It would also be possible to see in this remark a premonitory insight into the development of his own work.

He was to become acquainted with Corot, and was never to forget a remark by that artist which corresponded so well to the ambiguities of his own art: « Next to an uncertainty, place a certainty. » Corot's influence was to be seen in the treatment and tonality of his early landscapes.

As for Gustave Moreau, Redon praised him, but valued his watercolors above all – which is indicative of a sound judgment on this painter. We shall later investigate to what extent Redon's painting sometimes closely resembled, and especially how it differed from, Moreau's work.

When we reflect on what Redon's vision was later to be, and on those magical bouquets in which he seems to have been possessed by the secret of the fascination of each individual flower, his first youthful friendship, the one that linked him with the botanist Armand Clavaud, appears to be of major importance. Such meetings are worthy of greater attention than certain facts of a professional nature which nourish the biography of an artist without shedding light on those mysterious paths by which, unknown to him, he advances toward the suddenly decisive stage of his development. We can therefore refrain from lingering over Redon's attempts to join the École des Beaux-Arts, his failure in the entrance examination, and his brief and for him so-disappointing sojourn in Gérôme's studio, noting only the young artist's basic hostility to all official instruction.

Armand Clavaud was carrying on work in plant physiology, and was interested in the most minuscule plants and in that intermediate and disquieting life between the animal nature and the plant. Redon seems to have later illustrated and transfigured this preoccupation in the composition of certain works in which there unfolds a kind of dream of vegetation animated by an ambiguous life. Clavaud possessed an extremely broad culture, and his passion for literature was contagious. It was through him that Redon learned of Flaubert, Baude-

ROSE IN A VASE, 1865-1867 Oil, 18″ × 13½″ Musée des Beaux-Arts, Algiers

11

THE CLIFFS AT VALIÈRES, 1900   Oil, 11½″ × 17¾″
Arï Redon Collection, Paris

12

laire, and Edgar Allan Poe, all three of whom were later to serve as the inspiration for some admirable lithographs.

Another very important encounter for Redon was his meeting with Rodolphe Bresdin, who initiated him into engraving and lithographic work. He made his acquaintance around 1863 in Bordeaux, where the prodigious engraver, whose work was to remain for so long misunderstood, was living in extreme misery. For the first time Redon saw an artist place the resources of a very confident technique at the service of an imagination fertile in dreams and delirium. Bresdin never worked from nature. He knew how to look at it, however, and in his fantastic landscapes, in which the vegetation was depicted with an abundance of inextricable details (« detailed to the point of madness, » in the words of Théodore de Banville), and in which, again, a certain ambiguity sometimes reigned over apparitions that were more or less human or animal, mystery and drama took on the accent of a deeply felt truth.

In such works, that which Redon dimly perceived concerning an art sufficiently free to lead nature beyond her tangible reality, and which he had not yet dared to express himself, seemed to be a confirmation of his determination to follow the road he was to take. Redon signed *The Ford,* one of the first etchings he did in 1865, « pupil of Bresdin, » and the homage he paid the latter almost a half-century later, in the course of a lecture given in Holland, proves that he had always retained a faithful gratitude and fervent admiration for his master.

A universe in black and white

It was around 1862 that Odilon Redon began to paint. Still extant are *Flowers* (1865), a *Self-portrait* (1867), and a few slightly later studies of Médoc landscapes. But these were only the timid first stages in an apprenticeship the necessity of which was not to force itself upon him until much later. At this time color did not in truth appear to him to be a satisfactory means of expressing what he had to say. His vision of the world acquired the plenitude of its mysterious power only when cloaked in those twilight shadows evoked by black and white. This is why, for him, unlike many other painters, drawing was not a mere exercise of observation or the temporary symbol to which the premeditated work is reduced. For more than thirty years, drawing was to represent for Redon the principal achievement of his creative power.

In his early charcoal drawings, a somewhat romantic atmosphere envelops the landscapes and continues to betoken the influence of Corot. Soon, however, his compositions take on a more serious note, and gradually they are oriented toward scenes into which there creeps an unobtrusive strangeness resulting

13

14   *The Gnome, around 1875   Charcoal, 18″ × 14½″*
Art Institute of Chicago

A Mask Tolls the Knell, 1882   Lithograph («To Edgar Poe»), 10¼" × 7½"   15
National Library, Print Room, Paris

CLOSED EY
18
C
15″ × 11
Mu
du Louv
Pa

◁
*Self-Portrait,
around 1888
Charcoal,
13½″ × 9″
Collection J.E.
van der Meulen,
The Hague*

Budd
unda
Pas
35½″ × ?
Priv
Collecti
Pa

◁

PORTRAIT
OF MADAME
REDON
EMBROIDERING,
1880
Pastel,
20″ × 14″
Arï Redon
Collection, Paris

MEDITATION, 1893 Pastel, 8″ × 6½″ Gallery La Boëtie, Serger Collection, New York

more from the way the plays of shadow and light are organized than from the subjects depicted. In this period Redon uses chiaroscuro as an essential method of expression. A remark by him stresses its importance in his work: « I insist on the fact that my entire art is limited solely to the resources of chiaroscuro, and it also owes a great deal to the effects of abstract line, that power drawn from deep sources which acts directly upon the mind. » We shall later see how Redon was to utilize this « power drawn from deep sources » not only in his drawings but also in his painting.

However, his charcoal drawings were to find the principal nourishment for their subjects in a fantastic world which he was to depict with the lucidity of a visionary, paying to the phantasms of his imagination the same scrupulous attention he would have paid them had they been real phenomena that had appeared before him, and drawing them with the same precision he used in drawing a face or a tree. This permitted him to state that « I cannot be denied the credit of giving life to my most unreal creations. » These creations were often monsters. But what Redon was seeking, and what strikes us in these unusual apparitions, is, above and beyond the terrifying aspect of these cyclopes and chimeras and the *Spider* with the human smile, the shadowy universe to which they seem to belong and with which we suddenly feel ourselves in communication, as if it were the projection before our eyes of our own most anguished dreams. Redon never sought to astonish us, but he had the gift of sweeping us, with a gentleness made spellbinding by the velvety substance of the charcoal, into the depths of a revery in which the most mythical scenes became perceptible and familiar to us. Such was the power which he himself admitted he possessed (without explaining it) when he said that his entire originality consisted « in causing improbable beings to live in human fashion according to the laws of the probable. »

It has been possible to see in Redon, not incorrectly, a precursor of Surrealism, for certain of his drawings are composed of an unexpected meeting of elements that express the freedom of spirit with which he juxtaposed the objects of real life and those of the dream life on the paper. In *Eye with poppy*, for example, a large, carefully drawn eye, surmounted by a poppy close to a leaf or a feather which has loomed up in space, stands out against a rectangle of light that evokes a sky seen in the frame of a window. Elsewhere, human heads take wing among the clouds. But even when the exceptional is less obviously presented, something in Redon's compositions always rivets our attention by its character of enigmatic gravity. *Woman seen in profile*, whose face is turned toward strange forms that are only just floral (they belong, in truth, to the pure domain of abstraction), seems to be tinged by a disquiet that turns our contemplation into an inquiry. Thus a question is always raised in Redon's works, and we should be careful not to seek an answer. While he

The Eye, a Strange Balloon, Moves Toward the Infinite, 1882   Lithograph («To Edgar Poe»),
10¼" × 7¾" Collection Galerie Le Bateau-Lavoir, Paris

The Raven, 1882 Charcoal, 15¾″ × 11″ National Gallery of Canada, Ottawa

narrowly opens a door onto the mystery, he nevertheless does not give us the power to enter it.

Redon continued the exploration of this « obscure world of the *indeterminate* » – for which he hoped, he says, « to produce in the spectator a kind of diffuse and dominant attraction » – in his lithographs, at first out of a simple desire to multiply his charcoal drawings, as was the case with his first series of plates, *In the dream*, published in 1879, and then out of enthusiasm for a technique in which he was constantly discovering new resources that served to enrich his black-and-white work. « All my plates, from first to last, have been simply the fruit of an inquisitive, attentive, anxious, and passionate analysis of that which the lithograph crayon, assisted by the paper and the stone, contained in the way of power of expression. »

The choice of themes treated in his lithographic series is clearly significative of the spirit climate in which the artist was developing his work. In 1882 he dedicated an album of six plates « To Edgar Poe. » We should not try to find in them an illustration of texts by the American writer; the are merely representative of a state of mind that harmonizes with the poet's penchant for the extraordinary. An example is the composition entitled *The eye, like a strange balloon, moves toward the Infinite*. Eyes always held a special fascination for Redon, whether by their gaze, in which scarcely the secret of a thought is revealed, or by the still more secret thought they conceal beneath their lowered lids. Several of his drawings and canvases bear the title *The closed eyes*, and he frequently presents the faces of his Ophelias, Eves, Orpheuses, Christs, and Virgins with closed eyes, a world asleep or enveloped in a solitude in which, it seems, he wished merely to suggest the interior presence of a dream.

In *The origins*, a series of eight lithographs published in 1883, an eye, inscribed in a question mark, is again the subject of a plate entitled *There was perhaps a preliminary vision tested in the flower*. The ambiguity of the plant kingdom formulated here reappears in the *Homage to Goya*, published in 1885; one of its six plates bears the notation *The marsh flower, a sad and human head*. In his other collections of lithographs – *The night* (1886), *Dreams* (which he dedicated in 1891 to the memory of his friend Armand Clavaud), and the three series of *The temptation of Saint Anthony*, published between 1888 and 1896 – a disturbing fauna stands side by side with an anxious humanity, wandering in a sublunar world over which the shadow of death persistently hovers.

Redon had settled in Paris after the Franco-Prussian War of 1870, in the battles of which he participated. Every summer, however, he returned to Peyrelebade, where the atmosphere, the silence, and the memories of his unsociable childhood put him in a frame of mind so favorable to his work that no other place succeeded in arousing in him the feeling of the need to draw. He had need of this solitude, in which he could feel he was living « in a secret depth. »

24

The Red Boat, 1900 Oil, 35″ × 51¼″ Private Collection, Paris

Several submissions to the Society of Friends of the Arts of Bordeaux had been his only attempts to make himself known prior to 1881, when he exhibited his charcoal drawings for the first time in Paris, in an exhibition organized in the editorial offices of *La Vie Moderne*. It went almost unnoticed. Huysmans said a few words about it in an article, comparing Redon with Gustave Moreau and confining himself to a definition of his work in a formula that was too narrow to carry the weight of a judgment: « It is a nightmare carried over into art. » The fact is that no one had perceived, behind the unusual nature of the subjects, the admirable work of the draftsman, nor by what sobriety of method he achieved such a great expressive power. But Huysmans retained such a strong impression of his work that he selected some charcoal drawings by Redon to decorate the walls of the home of Des Esseintes, the neurotic hero of his *A' rebours*, published three years later. It can be said that he thereby paid the artist a tribute, even if he gave a description of his charcoal drawings excessively dramatized by the desire to stress their fantastic and frenzied aspect. But at the same time he distorted their character by forcibly enrolling Redon in the ranks of Symbolism and in according to him the dubious admiration of Des Esseintes, whose tastes similarly led him to venerate the work of Gustave Moreau.

This was an explanation which unfailingly influenced the judgment of Redon's contemporaries and warped it by placing his art under the dominance of a literature which thus appeared to have played a much more important role in his work than was actually the case. There is no disputing the fact that a relationship can be observed between certain compositions by Redon and those of Gustave Moreau. But though both artists sometimes felt a preference for the same themes, Redon never permitted himself to be seduced by that esthetics of the oriental tale, that baroque mythology, and those ornamental refinements into which Gustave Moreau had ventured. Moreau never succeeded in introducing into his works an idea of mystery other than in a theatrical form; he never achieved that poetic depth into which Redon had the gift of leading us, and which came not from a display of symbols and allegories but very simply from a manner of seeing and of expressing himself.

Moreover, Redon always denied that he had developed his works with literary, mystical, or metaphysical intentions. Yet he could not be satisfied with the mere depiction of external objects. He could have adopted for his own Hegel's observation that « the chief determinant of the content of painting is that of subjectivity in itself ». This corresponded closely to the thought he himself expressed in prophetic fashion when he noted in his Journal that « the future belongs to the subjective world. » This explains the criticisms he had formulated with regard to the Impressionists. In his eyes they did not sufficiently take into consideration that which was essential for him, namely, « everything

THE SHULAMITE, 1897   Lithograph, 9¾″ × 7½″   Private Collection, Paris

THE RED BUSH, 1901   Oil, 21¾″ × 18″   Private Collection, Paris

that surpasses, illuminates, or amplifies the object, and elevates the mind into the region of the mystery, the anxiety of the unresolved...., all that our art contains in the way of the unexpected, the vague and the undefinable, and that gives it an appearance which verges on the enigma.... »

At that time it was not easy to win public acceptance for a conception that was opposed both to the academicism of the Salons (where Redon's submissions were refused) and to forms of expression which, like Impressionism, were themselves opposed, in a different way, to this academicism. However, this won him the friendship of a small group of writers and artists — notably Mallarmé, and, later, Bonnard, Vuillard, and Maurice Denis — who very quickly recognized the worth of his personality. The independence of his position, which kept him outside all the esthetic movements of his time, ultimately led him to found, in 1884, the Salon des Indépendants, of which he was the first president.

Discovery of color

The diligent pursuit of his black-and-white work (charcoal drawings, lithographs, more rarely etchings, and numerous drawings in plumbago and India ink) was not to divert Redon completely from his pictorial studies. But the original work by which he established himself as a great painter was not achieved until after the closing years of the century, when he was already over fifty years of age.

The differences between the early landscapes of the Peyrelebade region and canvases executed some fifteen years later (i.e., around 1880), for example, the *Port in Brittany*, are not very pronounced, although the painter had acquired a more confident technique and his palette had become more varied and more sensitive. But it continued to be subdued and, as it were, confined to a tonality which would not by its brilliance repudiate his preference for the gray harmonies of charcoal. This is the case with his first pastel, *Portrait of Madame Redon embroidering*, which dates from 1880, the year of his marriage. The beautiful bent head, seen in profile, barely emerges from the shadow in which the hair and the dress blend into a single dark color, the lighting of the face occupying just enough space to illuminate its expression of gentle gravity.

By virtue of its substance, very similar to that of charcoal, the pastel was for Redon, at this period, certainly an intermediate stage between drawing and painting. Above all, he was to find in it, without deviating from a technique that was familiar to him, the encouragement to overcome the distrust that color still seemed to arouse in him. Nevertheless, he did not immediately utilize it for the mysterious, personal themes that made the originality of his drawings so engaging.

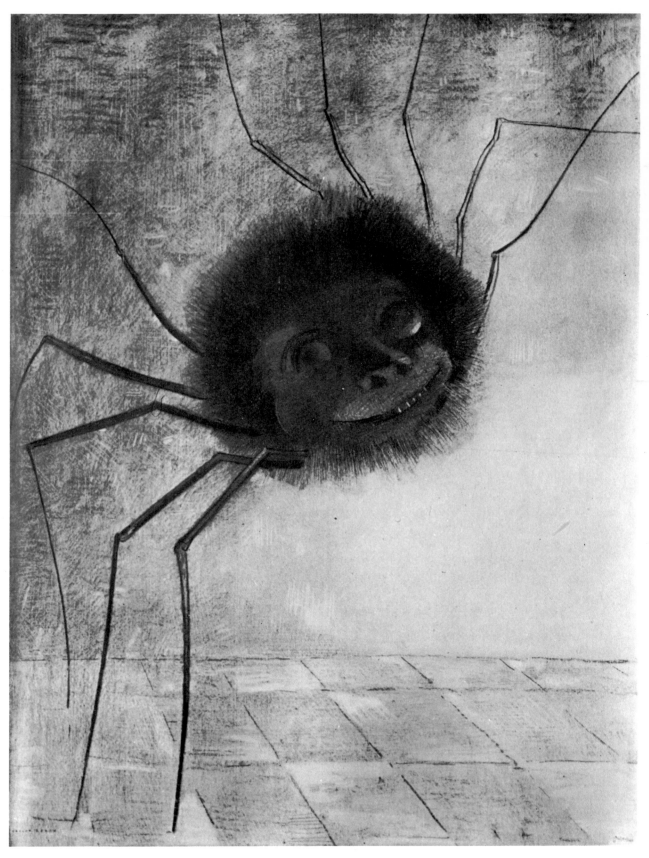

Martyr's Head, around 1894   Charcoal, 14½" × 14¼"
Kröller-Möller Rijksmuseum, Otterloo, The Netherlands

The Smiling Spider, 1881   Charcoal, 19½" × 15½"
Louvre, Cabinet des Dessins, Paris

Madness, 1877   Charcoal, 14¼″ × 12¼″   Claude Roger-Marx Collection, Paris

Intuition (or Mephisto), 1877   Charcoal, 15½″ × 13½″   Private Collection, Switzerland

*There Was Perhaps a Preliminary Vision Tested
in the Flower, 1883
Lithograph (« Les Origines »), 10¼" × 7¾"
National Library, Print Room, Paris*

*Flower with a Child's Head, around 1885
Charcoal, 15¾" × 12¾"
Art Institute of Chicago*

Suit of Armor, 1891 Charcoal, 20" × 14¼" Metropolitan Museum of Art, New York

The Wall Opens and a Death's Head Appears, 1887
Lithograph («The Juror») 9¼" × 7"   Art Institute of Chicago

37

Profile of Light, 1881-1886 Charcoal, 15" × 11" Private Collection, Paris

Eye with Poppy, 1892   Charcoal, 18″ × 12½″   Claude Roger-Marx Collection, Paris

In 1886, the same year in which his participation in the exhibition of the Salon des XX in Brussels won him the admiration of the entire artistic and literary avant-garde of Belgium, we find Redon appearing in the eighth Salon des Impressionnistes. This may seem surprising, when we know that he did not admit to any esthetic fellowship with the painters of this school. But we must take into consideration the fact that in 1886 the last exhibition of the group no longer presented any significant cohesion. Monet and Renoir had refrained from participating, and while Sisley and Pissarro were still with the group, painters of such differing tendencies as Degas, Gauguin, and Forain were also to be seen, as were Seurat and Signac, both of whom, like Redon, exhibited there for the first time. Odilon Redon was in truth to take a path clearly opposed to Impressionism, and was to accomplish the work which was gradually, with that slowness imposed on all true creators, to ensure his fame.

One of the first canvases in which there appears, still quite subdued but in an already impressive manner, that indefinable character of strangeness which Redon had ultimately carried over from his charcoal drawings into his painting is *The Arab musician* (usually called, incorrectly, *The Arab with the guitar*), which dates from 1893 and which hangs in the Petit Palais. In the center of the picture, a small, bright red figure playing an instrument which is not a guitar stands out against a background that represents no definite place; it can only be described as a surface with partial impastos in which the strokes of color are laid on according to a technique that today would be called *tachist*. On this canvas, evocative of a strange blend of Delacroix and Monticelli, there is thus nothing but this figure lost in the purely abstract world of the disappearance of objects. The singularity of such a composition resides precisely in the inexplicable (at least at first) relationship between the red Arab and the intangibility of that which surrounds him, a relationship very representative of the ambiguity of spaces which will be found so frequently in Redon's vision.

But what we call « vision » in a painter is also a technical particularity, since the « way of seeing » exists only insofar as it becomes discernible in a « way of painting. » This is very striking in the backgrounds conceived by Redon: he found the means to make us see something without showing us anything. He was able to bring to his brushstrokes of paint an idea of the « possible » that intrigues our way of seeing. Our eyes seek to clarify the nature of this space which evades our grasp — a desert-like stretch, the surface of an ocean, a sky veiled with clouds? — and which appears to us in turn near and far, solid and imponderable, as fleeting as a thought or a mirage, and always infinite. Every object placed in contact with this uncertain space then becomes itself an object of uncertainty. A figure, a face, a bouquet are shown to us only in the instant of an ephemeral apparition, outside of time, and we expect to see them suddenly disappear.

HOMAGE TO GAUGUIN, 1904   Pastel, 24½″ × 20″   Private Collection, Paris

THE HOUSE AT PEYRELEBADE, 1895-1897
Oil, 14″ × 17″   Arï Redon Collection, Paris

THE ARAB MUSICIAN, 1893
Oil, 20″ × 17¼″   Petit Palais, Paris

43

THE LEMON AND THE PEPPER, 1901   Oil, 10″ × 19″
Mrs. Bonger, Collection, Almen, The Netherlands

THE CYCLOPS, 1898   Oil, 25″ × 20″
Kröller-Möller Rijksmuseum, Otterloo, The Netherlands

THE GREEN DEATH, 1905-1910 Oil, 22¾″ × 19″ Mrs Bertram Smith Collection, New York

MAN WITH SERPENT, around 1907 Oil Private Collection

◁
PORTRAIT
OF ARÏ, 1897
Pastel,
18″ × 12½″
Art Institute
of Chicago

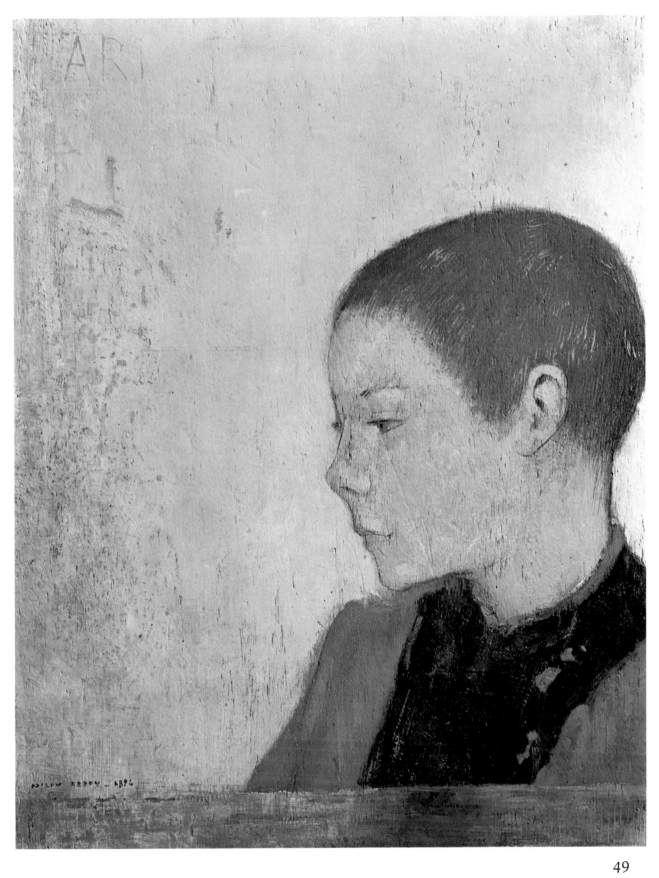

49

50   PORTRAIT OF MADAME REDON WITH A YELLOW SCARF, around 1890   Pastel, 26″ × 20″
Kröller-Möller Rijksmuseum, Otterloo, The Netherlands

PORTRAIT OF MARIE BOTKIN, 1900   Red chalk, charcoal and pastel, 25″ × 19″   51
Arï Redon Collection, Paris

52

THE FLIGHT INTO EGYPT, around 1902   Pastel and gouache, 20″ × 24″
Private Collection, New York

THE SACRED HEART, around 1895   Pastel, 23½″ × 17¾″
Musée du Louvre, Paris

ORPHEUS, after 1903   Pastel, 27½″ × 22¼″   Cleveland Museum of Art

JEANNE CHAINE, 1903   Pastel, 31¼″ × 27¼″   Basel Museum

ROGER AND ANGÉLIQUE, around 1910   Pastel, 35¾″ × 28″   Museum of Modern Art, New York

For Redon, pastel became in turn, around 1895, a freer and more powerful method of expression, in which the figures escaped from the somber universe of his drawings suddenly appear in bright light with their burden of fatality and tragedy. There is, for example, the *Veiled woman* in the Kröller-Müller Rijksmuseum, which is handled with very great economy of means, and which seems halfway between disdain and bitterness.

Redon was henceforth in possession of a new power he had discovered in color. He was undoubtedly quite conscious of it when he suddenly and completely gave up his *noirs* in 1897, after the sale — so painful for him — of the old family home at Peyrelebade. The end of the estate coincides with the end of a period of his life as well as a period of his art. A new Redon was coming to birth. This new Redon, a colorist enamored of light, seeking to express a certain height of happiness by the depiction of themes he had never attempted and by harmonies of tints whose freshness and brilliance are for him a kind of discovery of himself, was to be the painter of the enchanted bouquets, of the *Chariot of Apollo* and the *Birth of Venus*. The eyes plunged for so long into the uncertainties of the night were now opening on other uncertainties — for light itself possessed its own mysterious charms for Redon — but they had lost their threatening powers in the warmth of the sun.

One of the themes that was to reappear frequently in his painting after 1900 is that of the *Red boat*. One of his first canvases bearing this title is also one of Redon's largest paintings (35 inches by 51¼ inches). It is distinguished from those which were to be painted at a later date by a darker coloration. The red of the boat gradually takes on the character of a genuine incandescence that extends to the figures on board, as in the *Red boat* in the collection of Mme. Jäggli-Hahnloser. Between the sea, almost flowery, like a field in spring, and the sky, in which pink and gold clouds diffuse their cheerful light, the brilliant red of the boat, made to seem even more intense by the blue of the sails, is the unusual and disturbing typically Redonesque element that carries this entire seascape into a semi-imaginary domain. This was always to be the case in Redon's canvases. A detail, a color, a flash suffice to challenge a portion of nature's material reality. It appears, as it were, through that « invisible wall » which, according to Schelling, separates « the real world from the ideal world. » Here the painter joins the philosopher when he himself writes that the artist should have his eyes open « to the two worlds of life, to two realities which it is impossible to separate. »

Faithful to this esthetics of ambiguity, Redon, just as he leads nature to the border between the real and the unreal, introduces into his mythical evocations the realistic detail by which myth preserves a link with terrestrial manifestations. Venus, Andromeda, Orpheus, and Apollo appear in mythical land-

58   *The Gambler, 1879 Lithograph (« In the Dream »), 10½″ × 7¾″*
National Library, Print Room, Paris

The Prisoner, before 1897   Charcoal, Private Collection   59

Horse, around 1883   Charcoal, 16½″ × 15½″
Jacques Dubourg Collection, Paris

PHAËTHON'S CHARIOT, around 1900   Pastel, 19″ × 22¾″
Stedelijk Museum, Amsterdam

61

THE DREAM, around 1904   Oil, 22¼″ × 17″   Private Collection, Fribourg, Switzerland

THE RED SPHINX, 1910-1912   Oil, 24″ × 19½″   Professor Hans R. Hahnloser Collection, Bern

FLOWERS ON BLANK GROUND, 1905 Pastel, 15¼″ × 12½″ Private Collection, Paris

Portrait of Pierre Bonnard, 1902   Lithograph, 5¾″ × 4¾″
National Library, Print Room, Paris

The Reader (portrait of Bresdin), 1892   Lithograph, 12¼" × 9¼"
National Library, Print Room, Paris

The Torch, around 1880   Charcoal 12¾″ × 11¼″   Stephen Higgins Collection, Paris

scapes without any loss of the human quality of their happiness or unhappiness. In the very beautiful pastel *Orpheus* in the Cleveland Museum, Orpheus (a theme very often chosen by Redon) sleeps a mortal sleep on the side of a mountain that seems to welcome him with all the power of Earth. He is watched over by humble flowers under a sky barely darkened by violet shadows, while fawn-colored flashes bathe the strange composition in a kind of comforting warmth.

In the late work of this painter, who seemed to discover the joy of living on the threshold of old age, all sadness is thus transcended by a secret hope. And when it is pure joy that he is painting, as in the dazzling *Birth of Venus* in the Petit Palais, in which the shell actually seems to have become flesh (both are painted in the same ocher tone), a great festival of colors comes to life under the blue sky in a rhythm whose movements have been, as it were, inspired by water and fire, and which surrounds Venus with a cheerful excitement. In another work of the same title (the one in the Stephen Higgins collection), painted two years later, in 1912, the body of Venus, still enclosed in its shell like a beautiful fruit of flesh in its pearly skin, rises in a vertical line which is accentuated by the elongated shape of the canvas, thus giving the impression of a thrust toward the sky pushing up from the bottom of the sea. Its colors are still more joyful, and an ethereal lightness is imparted to it by the somewhat sifted lighting of the central motif, in which pink predominates.

In the same year, Redon executed one of his most beautiful pastels, modeled on a shell that Ary Leblond had brought him from the Seychelles. *The shell* (this time without Venus) and its model are still in the apartment on the Avenue de Wagram in Paris where he settled in 1905 and where his son Arï still lives amid the souvenirs of his father which he has piously preserved. Here again the relationship between the object depicted and its background, the precise draftsmanship of the one and the misty coloring of the other, the feeling of delicacy and the mystery it emits, leave us incapable of explaining this secret power that Redon possessed of translating the simplest things into a genuine poetic language, but they convince us that the technique had never before been carried so far. He had also used it between 1905 and 1910 (it has not been possible to ascertain the exact date) for a work which, it is true, remained isolated, but which nevertheless shows how far Redon had advanced in the search for a style of expression which no one had as yet explored. This work, *Plays of colors*, is, as its title modestly proclaims, a pastel in which, by the juxtaposition of forms difficult to identify with objects, color is taken as the subject of the composition. A decision so daring for that period should not greatly surprise us in this painter; as we have seen in his charcoal drawings, many of his canvases display an area of abstract forms that participate in the indeterminate nature of his vision. Such is the case in *The red sphinx*

68

THE DREAM (detail), around 1912   Oil   Madame L. Jäggli-Hahnloser Collection, Winterthur, Switzerland

ÉVE, 1904   Oil, 24″ × 18″   Jacques Dubourg Collection, Paris

Monk Reading (or Alsace), 1905-1909 Oil, 25½″ × 21″ Kunstmuseum, Winterthur, Switzerland

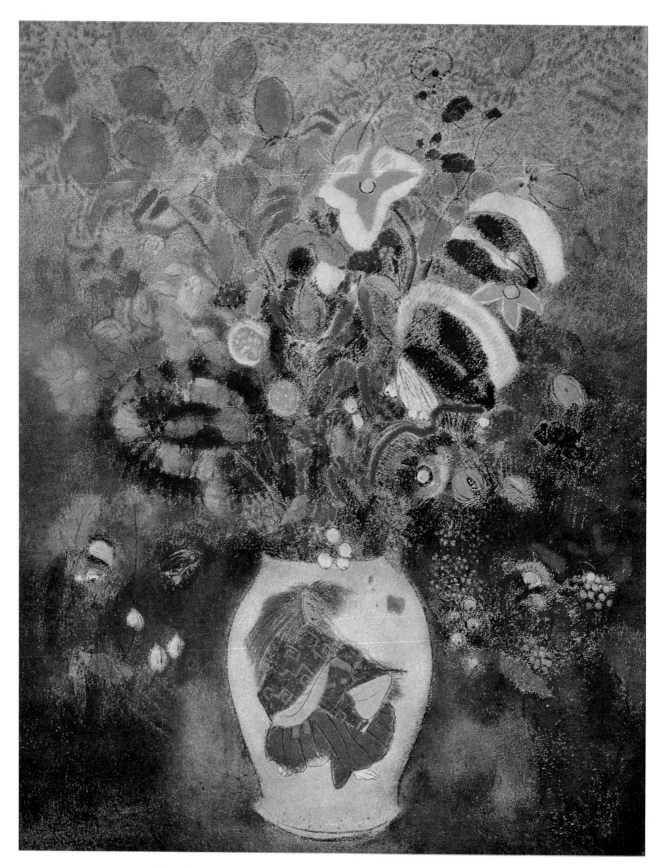

THE JAPANESE WARRIOR VASE, 1905-1908 Pastel, 36¼ × 28¼
Private Collection, Paris

LARGE BOUQUET OF FIELD FLOWERS, around 1912 Pastel, 32¼″ × 24″
Professor Hans R. Hahnloser Collection, Bern

THE SHELL, 1912   Pastel, 19″ × 22″
Arï Redon Collection, Paris

WOMAN AMID FLOWERS, 1909-1910   Pastel, 26″ × 22″
Mrs. H. Harris Jonas Collection, New York

THE BATTLE OF THE CENTAURS, around 1912   Oil, 20″ × 25½″
Jacques Dubourg Collection, Paris

RED BOAT WITH SUN, undated Oil
Private Collection, The Netherlands

77

THE DREAM, around 1912   Oil, 28¼″ × 21¾″
Madame L. Jäggli-Hahnloser Collection, Wintherthur, Switzerland

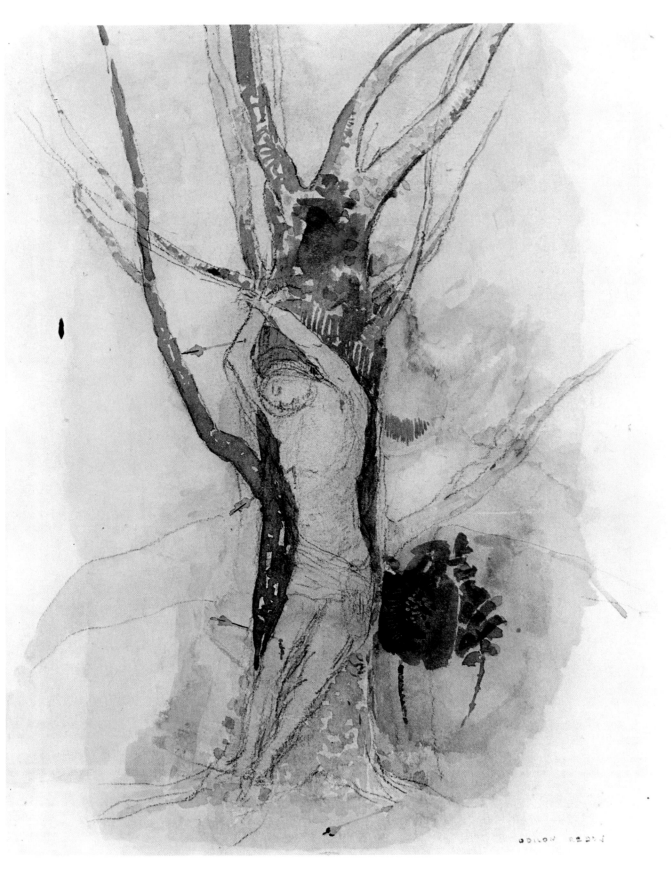

Saint Sebastian, 1910   Watercolor, 10″ × 7¼″   Musée des Beaux-Arts, Basel

RED BALL, 1910   Oil, 8½″ × 6¼″   Private Collection

in the Hans R. Hahnloser collection, where color seems to be captured in the moment of a metamorphosis that is transforming it into mist, a flower, or a butterfly.

For Redon, flowers were always a subject for study as well as an object of the dream. They traverse his work with an almost obsessive persistence. Sometimes they loom out of the depths of the sky, an oneiric garden in which the painter's mind wanders in pursuit of fleeting delights, as in *The dream*, in the collection of Mme. Jäggli-Hahnloser. The incorporeal profile of a woman with closed eyes, like an image of her own dream, is borne away among clouds, one of which has opened out into a sudden burst of flowers. Often, however, these flowers appear in simple bouquets arranged in a vase, which in no way detracts from their character as a miraculous apparition nor from the kind of human spirituality which seems to inhabit their plant form. Redon observed them in nature; sometimes he invented them, breathing into them a more intelligent life. Before certain of these paintings – for example, the *Bouquet of anemones* in the Petit Palais – we feel in fact that we are being *watched* by each flower; every one of them seems mutely to experience a desire to answer our question, to tell us an extraordinary secret, to reveal to us the significance concealed in the depths of its red or violet color.

Redon was not always aware of the imaginary form with which he endowed his flowers. One day one of his friends, Mme. Hedy Hahnloser, called his attention to the fact that one of his bouquets included flowers that did not exist in nature. He seemed surprised by this, and answered, « I didn't invent them – I see them that way. »

The *Bouquet of anemones* is a pastel with a square shape, i.e., one which is unusual in the history of painting. However, it is not exceptional for Redon. We discover it again in another pastel, the *Sea horses in an undersea landscape* (New Gallery, New York), in *The Engraver* (Petit Palais), and in a canvas in the collection of Hans R. Hahnloser, the *Feminine profile*, inscribed in a shell, an evocation of Mme. Redon, whose portrait the artist frequently did. For Redon was also a portraitist with a sensitivity that reflects the penetrating and, so to speak, analytical manner in which he was able to examine a face. The portraits of *Jeanne Chaine* (Basel Museum), *Violette Heyman* (Cleveland Museum), and *Marie Botkin* (Arï Redon collection), and that of *Gauguin* (Musée des Impressionnistes), which he painted from memory, reveal with what simplicity Redon achieved those nuances of expression that simultaneously reveal and conceal the model's thought. An extreme modesty, the note of a peaceful gravity, are for him essential elements of seduction in a woman, whose grace is in his eyes inseparable from a certain mystery. Thus he painted the admirable *Éve* of the Jacques Dubourg collection, a very little known work in which the reveries of a spirit in search of the feminine ideal are epitomized.

A Woman near a Tree, around 1894   Charcoal, 20½″ × 14½″
Jacques Dubourg Collection, Paris

A constantly growing body of work

The taste for simplicity, intellectual honesty, a constantly attentive charm, a modesty which, however, was not an unawareness of his personality, the feeling of moderation in all things, marked the life of Odilon Redon with a human quality appreciated by a his friends. We find the echo of this quality in the pages of the book *À Soi-même*, to which he consigned memories of his childhood and reflections on life and on his own art and that of others. Although he was sometimes astonished by the lack of understanding his works encountered, he felt neither bitterness nor anger. A wisdom which was the fruit of reflection, and the determination to accomplish his work in accordance with the goal he had set for himself ruled out any idea of revolt. This unobtrusiveness and lack of interest in the excitement and intrigues of life in Paris did not prevent him from gradually compelling recognition from a public which, it is true, was at first rather small, nor from attracting the attention of dealers and collectors.

Between 1889 and 1906, Durand-Ruel in Paris often exhibited his works. They could again be seen in Brussels in 1890, at the Salon des XX, and for the first time at The Hague in 1894. Ambroise Vollard in turn welcomed him to his gallery in 1898 and 1901, purchasing 102 charcoal drawings which are now dispersed in private collections. In 1904 an entire room was devoted to Redon at the Salon d'Automne. In the same year, *The closed eyes* was hung in the Musée du Luxembourg in Paris. In 1908, fifty-two of his works were exhibited at the Galerie Druet, and in 1913 he participated in an exhibition in Zurich and in the Armory Show in the United States. Also in 1913, André Mellerio published the catalogue of his engravings and lithographs.

Major patrons in turn appeared and demonstrated a touching fidelity to Redon. In 1900 he was commissioned to decorate the dining hall of the Château de Domecy in Burgundy; for this project he executed eighteen panels covering an area of 355 square feet. The following year he decorated the salon of Mme. Ernest Chausson. In 1903 he painted screens for Princess Cystria and for Olivier Sainsère. André Bonger, who began to purchase his paintings in 1892, and Gustave Fayet, for whom he decorated the library at Fontfroide in 1910, were among his first collectors. At Fontfroide (Aude), some seven miles from Narbonne, in a former Cistercian abbey which Gustave Fayet had purchased in 1908, the painter chose *Night* and *Day* as the themes of the two principal frescoes, each of which occupies an area 21½ feet long by 6½ feet high, and in which he retraced a kind of synthesis of the major stages in his own development.

Of all the private collections now including works by Redon, that of Mme. Bonger, at Almen in Holland, is the largest. It consists of seventy-eight: seventeen paintings, eleven pastels, three panels done in tempera *(Flowering tree, Red tree, Buddha),* one screen, twenty-one drawings, twenty-four lithographs, and one stained-glass window. The artist's favorite themes are represented here for the period ranging from 1864 to 1908, from his first studies of flowers down to those compositions in which, as the painter of an imaginary world and a spiritualized humanity, he was most profoundly himself: *Pegasus, Ophelia, Boat with holy woman,* and so on. It also includes a still life of 1901, *Lemon and pimento,* which shows us a little-known aspect of his work.

Another Redon collection, containing several of his most beautiful works, is the one which Mme. Hedy Hahnloser – who was a great friend of Bonnard, Vuillard, Matisse, and Vallotton – began to build up, with very knowledgeable taste, in 1912. This now belongs to her daughter, Mme. Lisa Jäggli-Hahnloser, in Winterthur, and her son, Professor Hans R. Hahnloser, in Bern. Their gracious homes in these two cities are genuine miniature museums, invaluable for the knowledge of the painting of the closing years of the nineteenth and beginning of the twentieth centuries.

Whereas the Franco-Prussian War had been for Redon an experience that was translated into a fecund awakening of his own creative powers, the war of 1914 was above all a great torment. In the continual state of anxiety in which he had been left by the departure of his son Arï for the front, it seemed to him that all happiness had come to an end forever. The time of friendly gatherings in which Bonnard, Vuillard, Maurice Denis, Émile Bernard, André Gide, Paul Valéry, Arthur Fontaine, Henri Kapferer, and so many others assembled at his home already belonged to a distant past which in effect was never again to come to life. In 1916, as the result of a chill, Redon was obliged to take to his bed, and he never got up again. He died on July 6, in his Paris apartment, at the age of seventy-six.

In his last years, despite the diminution of his powers and the anguished days of the war, the old painter had never abandoned his work. In 1914 he had made his last trip to Holland, where he had many friends. His last work, a *Profile of the Virgin,* in which the spiritual vision was tinged with melancholy, dates from 1916.

A few months after his death, a Russian collector, Jacques Zoubaloff, came to see Mme. Redon with the desire of becoming the owner of a work by the painter, for whom he had a deep admiration. He purchased the large pastel of *The Birth of Venus,* carried it away under his arm, hailed a taxi, and went straight to the Petit Palais to donate his acquisition. He often returned thereafter, and each time did the same thing with his purchases – pastel, watercolors, and drawings – thus building up in the Petit Palais the most remarkable collection of Redon works to be seen in Paris. « His works are too beautiful for me to want to keep them for myself, » he explained.

INCLINED FEMALE HEAD, around 1910 Watercolor, 8″ × 6½″ Arï Redon Collection, Paris

BOUQUET OF ANEMONES, after 1912   Pastel, 24½″ × 24½″
Petit Palais Museum, Paris

VASE OF FLOWERS, around 1914   Pastel, 29½″ × 23¼″
Petit Palais Museum, Paris

BIRTH OF VENUS, around 1910 Pastel, 32¾″ × 25¼″ Petit Palais Museum, Paris

Since then the fame of Odilon Redon has grown constantly and the most unrecognized aspects of his work have gradually been revealed in major exhibitions. Even today, however, it is not easy to acquire an extensive knowledge of his work. Dispersed throughout the world in numerous museums and private collections, the approximately two thousand works which he left in large part evade the most diligent organizers of retrospectives. The retrospective offered in Paris in 1956 at the Musée de l'Orangerie assembled only 213 works. And, while almost all his lithographs and engravings (Mellerio catalogued 206) are preserved in the Print Department of the National Library, few of his charcoal drawings are in public collections. (For a long time the Print Department of the Louvre Museum owned only one, but recent acquisitions permitted it to exhibit five in 1968 at the exhibition of the « Masters of black-and-white in the nineteenth century, from Prud'hon to Redon. ») But it is precisely in these charcoal drawings, in the always somewhat latent anxiety of their shadwy areas, sometimes clarified by a tragic accent, that we penetrate most deeply into the implication and virtualities of a body of work of which our understanding would remain incomplete if we were able to know only the creations that appeared in the sunlight of color.

The same is true to a certain extent of Seurat, whose conté crayon drawings are indispensable for a knowledge of the two aspects of his personality. In Seurat's work, however, and even though the crayon technique did not lend itself to the Neo-Impressionist methods of his painting, the graphic spirit remained very close to the latter, and the themes were the same. In Redon's work, on the other hand, the period which we could call « diurnal » in order to contrast it with the « nocturnal » period in fact stands opposed to the latter not only by the methods of realization but also by a complete renewal of the themes and their spiritual atmosphere.

The place that Redon's work has taken in the history of painting today seems to us all the more important in that it stands outside the great tributary movements of a theory or a school. In this way it affirms itself in all the power of its singularity. Though Redon sometimes flirted with the Symbolist ideology, and though he can be reproached, in his weakest compositions, with lingering over an esthetic that was an offshoot of that of the Pre-Raphaelites, he discovered is true originality elsewhere. That originality resides in the supreme liberty with which he translated into a single language and on to a single canvas both that which nature was able to offer him and also every invented form whose sources he ignored; it appeared before his gaze like the reflection of an interior scene whose elusive motifs he alone was capable of capturing.

In this way Redon, the precursor of the subjectivism of modern painting, was the painter of that dual reality that permitted him to attain the goal which

Paul Klee set himself in a different manner when he wished « to render a secret vision visible » while endowing visible objects with a secret depth.

Odilon Redon captured this silent universe which oscillates between night and day, between anguish and ecstasy, with its train of monstrous and divine beings, its improbable flora and fauna, its scenes in which the familiar stands side by side with the wondrous, this universe of the relative and the inexpressible that appears only by chance in our dreams and daydreams, in all its irrational truth, contributing to art a new expression of poetic thought.

Jean Selz

SUNSET, undated   Oil, 12″ × 17¾   Private Collection

BIOGRAPHY

1840. Odilon Redon, son of Bertrand Redon and Marie-Odile Guérin, is born on April 20 in Bordeaux. His childhood is spent at Peyrelebade (Gironde).

1855. Begins to study drawing with Stanislas Gorin.

1862. First charcoal drawings and paintings.

1863. Becomes friends with the botanist Armand Clavaud and with Rodolphe Bresdin. Nonmatriculated student in Gérôme's studio and the École des Beaux-Arts in Paris.

1867. Exhibits an etching (*The Ford*, 1865) at the Salon du Palais des Champs-Élysées.

1870-71. Participates as an ordinary soldier in the battles on the Loire. Settles in Paris after the war.

1874. Death of his father.

1875. Works in Barbizon and Brittany.

1878. First trip to Holland. First lithographs.

1879. Works in Brittany. Publishes his first lithographic album, *In the dream*.

1880. On May 1, marries Camille Falte, a half-sister of Juliette Dodu. First pastels.

1881. First exhibition of charcoal drawings at *La Vie Moderne* in Paris.

1882. Exhibits charcoal drawings, lithographs, and etchings in the exhibition room of the Parisian newspaper *Le Gaulois*.

1883. Works in Brittany.

1884. Exhibits at the first Salon des Indépendants, where he will exhibit again in 1886 and 1887. Becomes president of the Salon.

1885. Exhibits a lithograph at the Salon des Artistes Français.

1886. Birth and death of his son Jean. First participation in the Salon des XX in Brussels. Exhibits at the eighth and last Salon des Impressionnistes.

1888. Spends the summer at Samois.

1889. Birth of his son Arï. Spends the summer at Samois. Participates in the first exhibition of painters-engravers et Durand-Ruel in Paris, where he will exhibit every year until 1893.

1890. Goes to Brussels in February with Mallarmé, for the second exhibition of the Salon des XX, in which he participates.

1891. Exhibits at the General Exhibition of Lithography in the École des Beaux-Arts at Paris.

1894. Private exhibition in March-April at the Durand-Ruel Gallery. Exhibition at the Haagsche Kunstkring in Holland (May-June).

1895. Trip to London in October.

1897. Sale of Peyrelebade.

1898. Exhibits in Ambroise Vollard's gallery in Paris. Spends the summer at Saint-Georges-de-Didonne, near Royan, to which he will return every year for about ten years.

1899. Exhibition of young painters at Durand-Ruel Gallery, in honor of Redon. Publication by Vollard of his latest lithographic album, *The Apocalypse of Saint John*.

1900. Participates in the Centennial of French Art (Universal Exposition of Paris). Exhibits at Durand-Ruel. Trip to Italy with Robert de Domecy. Maurice Denis paints *Homage to Cézanne*, in which appear among others Redon, Bonnard, Vuillard, Roussel, and Sérusier (Musée National d'Art Moderne, Paris). Exhibits in Cracow.

1901. Exhibits at Vollard's gallery. Decorates the dining hall of the Château de Domecy, in Burgundy, and the salon of Mme. Ernest Chausson in Paris. Participates in the exhibition organized by Gustave Fayet at the Société des Beaux-Arts of Béziers.

1903. Redon is awarded the Legion of Honor. Exhibits at Durand-Ruel.

1904. The Salon d'Automne includes a Redon Room with sixty-two works. The Musée du Luxembourg in Paris acquires *The closed eyes*.

1905. Exhibits ten works at the Salon d'Automne.

1906. Exhibits at Durand-Ruel. Sends six works to the Salon d'Automne.

1907. Odilon Redon sale at the Hôtel Drouot. Trip to Switzerland. Exhibits three works at the Salon d'Automne.

1908. Trip to Switzerland. First tapestry cartoons for the Gobelins. Exhibits at the Galerie Druet in Paris.

1909. Settles in Bièvre (Seine-et-Oise) for the summer.

1910. Decorates the library of the Abbey of Fontfroide (Aude). In London, participates in the exhibition of « Manet and Post-Impressionism » at the Grafton Gallery.

1912. Participates in the Centennial of French Art at Saint Petersburg.

1913. Submits several works to the Exhibition of French Art at the Kunsthaus in Zurich. The International Exhibition of Modern Art (Armory Show) in New York, Chicago, and Boston includes a Redon Room (40 works).

1914. Exhibits at the Alfred Flechtheim Gallery in Düsseldorf. Trip to Holland.

1916. Redon dies on July 6 in Paris. Is buried in the cemetery at Bièvre.

★

1919. Redon exhibition at the Kunstmuseum in Winterthur.

1920. Redon retrospective (214 works) at the Galerie Barbazanges, Paris.

1923. Redon retrospective (300 works) at the Galerie Druet, Paris.

1926. Redon retrospective at the Musée des Arts Décoratifs, Paris.

1934. Redon exhibition at the Petit Palais, Paris.

1952. Redon exhibition (drawings and lithographs) at the Museum of Modern Art, New York.

1956. Redon retrospective (213 works) at the Musée de l'Orangerie, Paris.

1957. Redon retrospective (215 works) at the Gémeentemuseum, The Hague.

1958. Redon retrospective (210 works) at the Kunsthalle, Bern.

1959. Redon exhibition at the Mathieson Gallery, London.

1961. Redon exhibition at the Museum of Modern Art, New York.

1962. Redon exhibition at the Art Institute of Chicago.
Redon exhibition at the Venice Biennale.

1963. Redon exhibition at the Galerie Bernheim-Jeune, Paris.

1966. Redon exhibition (lithographs) at the Galerie Vallotton, Lausanne.

1967. Redon exhibition at The Hague Museum.
Redon exhibition at the Krugier Galleries, Geneva and New York.

1968. Redon exhibition at the Kunsthalle, Bern.

1969. Redon exhibition (drawings, etchings, lithographs) at the Galerie Le Bateau-Lavoir, Paris.

ODILON REDON'S WRITINGS

1868. *Le Salon de 1868.* Article in *La Gironde,* Bordeaux.

1869. *Rodolphe Bresdin.* Article in *La Gironde,* Bordeaux.

1894. *Lettre à Edmond Picard.* Published under the title « Confidences d'artiste » in *l'Art Moderne,* 34, Brussels.

1908. *Rodolphe Bresdin, 1822-1885.* Preface for the Bresdin retrospective at the Salon d'Automne, Paris.

1922. *A Soi-Même. Journal 1867-1915.* Ed. Floury, Paris, 1922. Ed José Corti, Paris, 1961.

1923. *Lettres d'Odilon Redon. 1878-1916.* Preface by M.-A. Leblond. Ed G. van Oest, Paris and Brussels.

1926. *Lettres à Emile Bernard.* La Rénovation esthétique, Tonnerre.

BIBLIOGRAPHY

1891. DESTRÉES, Jules: *L'Œuvre lithographique d'Odilon Redon.* Ed. Deman, Brussels.

1913. MELLERIO André: *Odilon Redon.* Society for the Study of French Engraving, Paris.

1913. PACH, Walter: *Odilon Redon,* New York.

1913. *L'Œuvre graphique d'Odilon Redon.* 2 vols. Artz and De Bois, editors. La Haye.

1923. MELLERIO André: *Odilon Redon, peintre, dessinateur et graveur.* Ed. Floury, Paris.

1925. ROGER-MARX, Claude: *Odilon Redon.* No. 21, « Les Peintres français nouveaux » series, N.R.F. Paris.

1929. FEGDAL, Charles: *Odilon Redon.* Ed. Rieder, Paris.

1950. ROGER-MARX, Claude: *Redon. Fusains (Charcoals).* « Plastique » series. Ed. Braun, Paris.

1955. SANDSTRÖM, Sven: *Le monde imaginaire d'Odilon Redon.* Ed. Gleerup, Lund.

1956. BACOU, Roseline: *Odilon Redon.* 2 vols. Ed. Pierre Cailler, Geneva.

1960. *Lettres à Odilon Redon* (from Gauguin, Gide, Huysmans, Jammes, Mallarmé, etc.). Ed. José Corti, Paris.

1964. SELZ, Jean: *Odilon Redon réveillé.* In *Le dire et le faire.* Ed. du Mercure de France, Paris.

1964. BERGER, Klaus. *Odilon Redon.* Ed. Du Mont Schauberg, Cologne.

1968. *Redon.* Text by R. Negri and Ch. de Bellescize. « Chefs-d'œuvre de l'Art » series. Ed. Hachette, Paris.

1970. *Odilon Redon à l'Abbaye de Font-froide.* Text by Roseline Bacou and Claude Roger-Marx. « Chefs-d'œuvre de l'Art » series. Ed. Hachette - Fabbri - Skira, Paris, Milan, Geneva.

ILLUSTRATIONS

95